MW01294568

Organize Your Closet

By Diane L. Worthy

ALL RIGHTS RESERVED. No part of this book may be reproduced or transmitted in any form whatsoever, electronic, or mechanical, including photocopying, recording, or by any informational storage or retrieval system without express written, dated and signed permission from the author.

Copyright © 2013 Published by Diane L. Worthy

Introduction

First Steps To Organizing A Closet......Page9

Organizing Bottoms, (Shorts, Pants, Trousers) In Your Closet......Page14

Organizing Dresses, Suits, Jackets and Expensive Clothing In Your Closet......Pg19

Organizing Shirts, Blouses, And T-shirts In Your Closet......Pg22

Organizing Shoes In Your Closet......Pg26

Organizing Other Accessories In The Closet......Pg29

How to Keep An Organized Closet Organized......Pg33

Additional Tips In Organizing Your Closet......Pg39

Introduction

Many people find it very difficult keeping the things they own in an organized way, which allows them to find what they require at any time they need it. The area that presents this challenge particularly is the closet.

The contents in a closet are out of sight immediately the doors are closed, so there is a risk of using the closet as a convenient place to stash items which are cluttering the main area of the house. This is an awful idea since it can make the closet a giant and vertical junk drawer.

If your closet is not organized, it is difficult to appear prepared. You are prone to dress in the same outfits many times with the same accessories. On the other hand, if a closet is organized, the morning routine is streamlined as well. You are more likely to locate more clothes and wear an ensemble that reflects your creativity and personality instead of your disorganization and tight schedule.

Once you are certain that you want to get your wardrobe in order, it is advisable to make a plan. You can choose to sketch a diagram of how you would like your items arranged, be specific on what you would like to have in each area of the closet.

Here are few tips to have your wardrobe work for you….

Storage Systems - A helpful tool in this case is a closet system. Closet systems are available in different shapes and sizes. The most basic closet systems are wire racks which are in built in the storage space. They provide horizontal hanging areas and shelf space.

There are more elaborate closet systems in the market; some can fit in the closet while others can simply stand against the wall on their own. They make the task of organizing a closet very easy, the down side is that they cost money.

If you don't desire to use money to get organized, you can make do with what you have at hand. Here are ways to organize closet in a cheap way;

Organization - Knowing what to wear and where to get it from greatly lessens the need to throw all clothes on the floor or bed. Organize the garments by type; sports, suits, casual and cocktails. Put all of the same kind of clothes together; skirts, undergarments, shorts, trousers and so forth. You can make it more appealing by arranging them according to color.

Visibility - Everything in your closet should be clearly visible and your best pieces should be the easiest to reach. This way, if you are running out of time, you can grab something reliable which makes you feel comfortable and smart.

Remix - Take a few minutes each week to find out some new combinations. The same outfit you wear occasionally would really look different when worn with something else different. It will also help you find some items in the closet that you have not worn in a while. The new items should now be placed where they can be easily seen.

Repair and Laundering - Do not keep items that need to be repaired or laundered in the closet. There is nothing as bad as pulling a shirt only to find the collar torn or with some stains. Before anything is arranged in the wardrobe, ensure that it is clean and can be worn at any time.

Be Selective - An important step is to have a review of the contents in the closet and empty what is not necessary. It is quite impossible to organize a small space that has too many things. A general rule states that at least 10% of the contents in each closet are disposable entirely.

Dispose of at least one item every week. Get rid of items more than the 10% if you can. The ultimate goal is to eliminate everything that does not serve you and donate it to a friend or charity. These items can be sold at a resale shop to earn you a few dollars. Things like storage boxes, suitcases and sport equipment take up too much space in the closet. Take these out as well and decide what or what cannot be allowed into the closet. Shoes, purses and storage items can be removed to make more room. The space under the bed can be used as a trunk to store these things instead of the closet.

Shelves - Shelves can be installed right in the middle for folded items like jeans, sweaters, t-shirts and pajamas. The shelves could be extended all the way up to the ceiling where there is space. They should deep enough to hold stacks of clothes that are not used as much. A divider right in the middle will help you include an organized closet.

Specialty Hangers - All accessories may be organized to cover the least room possible. Scarves, belts, ties, hats and even swimwear can be easily kept on a specialty hanger. A tie hanger, scarf and belt hangers can get rid of items off the shelves to make room for more items. These hangers are useful because they store several items. Hooks can be used inside the closet to hang more items. Space in between the hooks so that it is easy to access them and so that the closet does not look cluttered.

Space Saving Hangers - Slim line hangers are a life saver in any closet. They are super skinny and take up half the space of the other hangers. They also have a velvet coating which ensures that your clothes are firmly positioned in the hanger even when you rummage through the closet a lot. You can choose to piggy back these hangers to coordinate the outfits in the closet and save even more room. Pant hangers which hold a dew pairs of pants at a go are good in saving up of space too.

Internet - There are many ideas on the internet on how to organize closet. Many people have come with creative and beautiful ways to ensure that your closet is neat and easily accessible. Discover what options there are in the market these days. Many of them are actually very affordable and can be easily implemented.

All these can be implemented together to have an organized closet. If you are living a fast paced or hectic life, you owe yourself an organized closet. Keeping your closet in a proper organized shape can be a challenge but one you can be proud of. But with some patience and time you'll be able to find whatever you need when you need it. So what's the first step in getting your closet in order...?

First Steps To Organizing A Closet

Imagine an empty box. No one would see it pleasing, right? How about a box filled with clutter? I bet it's more of an eyesore. Closets are basically boxes that store our personal stuff. But unlike any other box, closets reflect our personality. How our closet looks like is what we really are deep inside.

Having an organized closet doesn't happen in an instant. Proper motivation and strong will to get things done are two of the most essential components needed. You must first convince yourself to commit to this endeavor. When you are 100% determined then get on with organizing.

Everything starts with planning. Action without proper strategy is a recipe for disaster. It's the same principle with organizing a closet. Starting right away without proper planning leaves you exhausted and your home still a mess.

When planning, one idea is to make a sketch of your own closet so that you'll have an idea on what items to put on this part and on that part, which space could be maximized and so on. Consider areas in your closet that need improvement. For example, if the topmost part of your closet is a mere vacant space, perhaps it's now time to stock your bags and other accessories there rather than hanging them somewhere else in the room which exposes them to dust and other agents that might cause damage.

You must have a clear picture of what you want to achieve in the end. This will help you identify things you will need along the way. Basic bits and pieces necessary in organizing closets include cleaning items and products to dust off and clean your closet, garbage bags for your clutter, huge boxes (if you've got stuff to give away or for you to store off-season clothes in), an air freshener, a pegboard for your accessories, durable hooks, collapsible plastic boxes for shoes, and hangers. Having the right materials at hand before getting to work will save your time and effort and ensures everything runs smoothly from the beginning.

When you're done with all the preparations, it's time to get your hands dirty.

Take all clothes out of the closet and those that are hung must be taken from their hangers. Fold the clothes neatly and pile them on the bed. Make sure all clothes are properly piled so that you'll be able to see which clothes should go back to the closet and which clothes should go to the off season/charity boxes.

In deciding which clothes to keep, here are some easy guidelines. Get rid of clothes that...

...do nothing for your appearance. Why save a space for this clothing it, this space could be used for better use?

...are outdated. Stop wearing clothes that were popular years ago but are outdated, unless you want to look like you've just gotten out of a time machine.

...do not fit you well. Clothes are supposed to make you feel comfortable and confident and not like "Dumbo" dressed in a ballerina costume or a walking skeleton wearing a XXXL shirt.

...you haven't worn in a century. If you are living in a warm climate and haven't worn a specific piece of clothing for more than half a year, then it's time to bid farewell to that item. If you're living in a changeable climate and haven't worn a specific clothe for more than a year, then it's time to dispose of it.

...don't represent who you are now. Wear something that best represents you. If you aren't the young person you were anymore why hold onto those clothes that don't represent who you are now. There's no use in keeping your hip-hop pants and extra-large jersey shirts if it's just not you any more.

...aren't comfortable. Clothes that make you itch or make you sweat like a pig must definitely go out of the closet. Also shoes that leave your feet hurting at the end of the day aren't really worth keeping anymore.

In other words, only wear clothes that you really need and that make you feel comfortable. Those that do not meet these standards must go somewhere else. And by somewhere else, I mean two things. One is the donation box and the other one is the storage/memory box.

Clothes that are not seasonally appropriate must be temporarily kept in your storage box to prevent congesting your closet. After all, who would wear furry coats in the summer? Also, you can keep items that hold special meaning to you such as your first prom dress given to you by your mom or your basketball jersey your father gave you. I understand that these items are dear to you but keep in mind not to hoard too many of these things. If you're finding it hard to part with these items why not clip off a sample or take a photo for a keep sake instead of hoarding the full sized item.

After sorting your clothes, make sure to arrange the boxes neatly. Label them properly so that you won't need to open them just to see what's inside. You may store them behind your closet or somewhere else in the house.

Donating clothes that you're not using may somehow be depressing but just think of the happiness it could give to the less fortunate. Those clothes may have not served their purpose to you but they can still serve their purpose to others. Your loss could be other's gain.

Now, it's time to clean up the closet. Start cleaning from the top to bottom of the closet. Sweep off all cobwebs and dust off the entire closet. Make sure that the closet is dry before putting back your clothes to it. If you think your closet is in need a face lift now could be the right time for a repaint or restructure your closet. You may want to add or remove some shelves, or perhaps you would like to put on a pegboard on the closet doors. You are the designer of your own closet. Just be careful in playing with the colors. Always put in mind that apart from aesthetics, accessibility, practicality, and functionality must be given high consideration.

Organizing Bottoms, (Shorts, Pants, Trousers) In Your Closet

How am I going to store my pants in the closet? Should I hang them all? What type of pants should be folded? I bet all these questions are running through your mind. Arranging your bottoms in the closet is not as easy as you think but if you take time and be patient in reading this chapter, you might soon find arranging your bottoms a piece of cake. Unlike what many of us think, not all bottoms are supposed to be hung. Among the list of bottom pieces you must hang are: skirts, denim pants/jeans, khakis, and slacks. Jogging/sweat pants, track pants, and pajamas are not meant for hanging. Since they are stretchable items, they tend to overstretch due to gravity over time, causing your bottoms to not fit you as well as they used to.

When hanging your pants, always keep in mind to allot space in between pants to allow airflow. Allowing the air to circulate prevents, if not avoids, presence of body odors and wrinkles. Further, you can easily spot the pants of your choice when they are evenly spaced. When you had your pants dry-cleaned, do not forget to remove your pants off the plastic bags before putting them in the closet. Aside from consuming a lot of space, plastic bags also obstructs proper airflow in the closet.

In addition, you must first take off the belt from your pants prior to hanging them. The weight of your belt causes distortion to the waistline. There are also some belts, especially the leather ones, which could cause permanent staining in the waistline once it has stayed there for too long. Any item, particularly those that are very bulky, must also be taken away from your pants' pockets. This could also cause distortion in your bottom piece.

Never hang inside your closet pants or bottoms that are still wet or moist. Doing so will promote growth of mildew or molds. Always remember that moist items are the best places for microorganisms and bacterial growth to happen especially when they are not exposed to air and sunlight. Therefore, proper airing out of your pants is a must before storing in the closet.

Do not store in your closet bottom pieces that are smelly. If you just came home from an exhausting routine jogging in your neighborhood, avoid hanging your pants back into the closet. This will make your closet smell awful. Likewise, if you're a smoker and your pants get coated with the smell of cigarette smoke, do not hang your pants in the closet unless you want all your closet items to smell this way.

If you have just arrived at home from a hectic day in the office, spare a little more time and effort to hang your pants. Do not leave on the floor in order to prevent unwanted creases to set in.

There are variations on how to hang your pants. For your office slacks, simply fold your pants following the creases and then fasten the top part. Do this in order to maintain a crisp fold. For your other pants that you want to maintain a flat front, hang them the way you wear them.

If you do not have the luxury of space in your closet to accommodate all bottom pieces in the hanging track, then fold your other bottom pieces like your jeans in a more presentable manner. Learn how to fold your pants as if they are saleable items in a wardrobe boutique.

Here are some simple steps that will guide you in folding your pants to save more space and end up with a visually pleasing closet.

Lay your jeans flat on a clean surface (e.g. the bed) and unwrinkle them using the palm of your hand. Fold them lengthwise, exposing the pocket located at the buttocks area. Fold the bottom part of the jeans by one third. Shape the jeans into square by folding the jeans going to the top. Now, the exposed back pocket is covered. Flip the jeans over to expose the other pocket. You're now ready to pile your jeans in the shelves of your closet. You can do the same with your trousers and shorts.

Here's a video on how to fold up your pants quickly and easily…http://bit.ly/162FnGV

If you have no shelves in your closet, you can always improvise. Pile your folded pants in a bin that you can place underneath your hanging pants. This will maximize your closet space.

Another important piece in your closet is the underwear. Contrary to what many people practice, they must not be placed in a box like assorted goodies. If you use drawers, suitcase or organizer boxes to store your undies, this is the type of folding you must apply:

Lay the underwear flat on a clean surface and even out creases. Fold one side going to the middle then do exactly the same on the opposite side. Fold the bottom part by one third and fold it once again going to the top to achieve a rectangular form.

Another way to store pants is in a simple plastic tube. Find a plastic tube ether of a small enough diameter that your underwear won't fall straight through and push your clean underwear inside. Using pipes this way is easy to use and you're guaranteed to use all your underwear rather than relying on only a small number or pants that get used over and over again. If you are using pipes to store your undies, another method of folding would be best for you. Lay down your undies flat and fold the band about an inch or two (depending on the size) toward the bottom part. Fold one side towards the midline and do the same on the other side. Grasp the top part then roll the bottom part toward the top. Pull the bottom part gently as you go up.

Pipes are creative tools in maximizing space in your closet. It's not just affordable, it's also genius.

Organizing Dresses, Suits, Jackets and Expensive Clothing In Your Closet

Basic principles still apply when storing your expensive clothes. Make sure they are clean and dry prior to storing in the closet. Dry cleaning should be done before storage especially when you plan no to use it for quite some time. Take off clothes from dry cleaning plastic bags to maximize space in the closet and in order to allow air to circulate. Airflow prevents setting in of permanent creases and growth of molds. Keep your closet well ventilated. It is advised to maintain at least an inch in between every item that is hung in your closet.

Avoid using offensive-smelling moth balls in your closet. Its smell tends to stick in your clothes. No one wants to smell as if you've lived inside a closet for decades. Instead, you may use cedar blocks to keep your designer clothes free from insects.

Make sure to take off any fashionable pin, brooches, and badge/emblem from your clothes. Keeping them pinned to your designer clothes for some time will damage the fabric and cause some distortion. Separate clothes that are filled with beads and sequins from your clothes made of fine fabrics like silk as this may accidentally cause tears or scratches in your expensive clothes.

Designer items that are quite heavy and stretchable, like your sweaters, must not be hung because they will stretch out. Instead, you should fold them neatly. To help you organize your designer clothes without jeopardizing their quality, you will need the right kind of hanger. I've listed some friendly guideline in choosing which hanger best works for this and that. Consider the size of the hanger. Lighter garments like dresses require a not so thick hanger. The most common would be a half inch-thick. On the other hand, heavier garments like suits, jackets and coats need an inch-thick hanger. Avoid using very large hangers that would overstretch the shoulders or too small hangers that would make your clothes appear limp.

Usually, for designer items, contoured hangers are used in order to maintain the shoulder's curvature. Flat hangers, on the other hand, are best to use for shirts in order not to congest the closet space. Generally, hangers are designed based on its function. There is really a specific hanger for every type of clothing. For example, hangers padded with satin are ideal for hanging lingerie and the like. The satin covering prevents hitches.

The size and space in your closet will also determine the type of hanger you must use. If you've got a small closet, choosing flat hangers would be a wise decision as they consume less space. If your closet is spacious enough and you care more about your expensive clothes, then you'll go for contoured hanger.

There are also some who pay more attention with aesthetics. If you want to project a nature-lover image through your closet, then go for wood hangers. This works better if your hangers match the material of your closet. For a modern touch, metal hangers would be a good choice.

For those who are on a tight budget, you could settle for the typical plastic hangers. Those who are more particular with eliminating or eradicating insects would probably choose cedar hangers. In addition, cedar hangers help protect the integrity of your expensive clothes by reducing moisture and stench in your closet.

Furthermore, taking care of your designer clothes does not only depend on how you organize them inside your closet. A huge percentage that predisposes expensive clothes to damage usually relies on the usage. If you tend to wear these clothes from time to time, then most probably they get damaged easily. Despite how much you love these items, learn to control yourself from wearing those over and over again. Constant wearing would mean constant washing or dry cleaning which in turn causes the fabric to weaken.

High quality clothes require high quality maintenance. You'll be saying goodbye to your thousands of dollars when you mistakenly put your designer clothes into the washing machine. Dry cleaning is recommended for these types of clothes.

Organizing Shirts, Blouses, And T-shirts In Your Closet

Tops commonly consume the largest space in the closet. There are lots of ways on how to maximize your closet space and one of those is by properly organizing your tops such as shirts, blouses, etc. You must also know which shirt must be hung and which one must not. Doing this will not only allow you to have a better-looking closet but more so, this will help prolong the "shelf-life" of your items.

Organizing clothes may somehow be confusing but the rule of thumb is: "choose the one that best works for you." In other words, organize according to your convenience but make sure it is neat and orderly. There are many ways on how to organize your clothes.

By season. If it's winter, hang first your winter clothes and perhaps your summer clothes can be folded for a while.

By type. For men, separate your long-sleeved shirts, short-sleeved shirts, polo shirts, round neck shirts, V-neck shirts, and sleeveless shirts from one another. Women may also do the same with their tank tops, blouses, etc.

By occasion. Your work clothes, casual, ragged and sporty clothes must be set apart from one another.

By frequency. Clothes that you frequently use must be placed in a more accessible spot in your closet. Those that are occasionally worn may be placed on a more distant part of the closet.

By color. A lot of people enjoy organizing their clothes when they do it according to color. You may do it from darkest to lightest shade. You may also follow the rainbow color pattern. Whichever best works for you.

Another interesting way of organizing your tops is by using color-coded hangers. You may use black hangers for your working clothes, white for your casual clothes and so on.

Make sure that there is enough space when hanging clothes to allow airflow to circulate and prevent wrinkling. Shirts must be buttoned up so that the collar won't sag and the neckline won't crease. Sleeves of heavy shirts must be crossed over the hanger so that it won't stretch. It is a must to hang suits, coats, button-down shirts, and blazers.

When hanging clothes, you must also put into consideration the type of hanger you have to use. Plastic hangers that are light in nature are best to use for lighter garments. Traditional suit hangers are ideal for specially tailored clothes, shirts made of linen, jackets, and coats. Wire hangers are among the most common hangers in the market however their use is not very much encourages because they tend to leave creases especially when used with pants. Also, they get rusty as time passes by.

Clothes that do not need to be hung may be folded and piled properly on your closet shelves. If you do not have shelves in your closet, you may use plastic bins and place them under your hanging clothes. By doing this, you can save more space.

The types of clothes that should be folded include heavy sweaters, t-shirts, underwear, knitted garments, and clothes that are made of stretchy material like nylon and spandex.

There are lots of styles when it comes to folding. But the style isn't really a big deal. What's important is that you lay down your clothe flat and free of creases before folding it. By doing so, you won't need to iron your clothes. You didn't only save your effort but also electricity.

Some prefer folding their clothes in a square form while others in a rectangular shape. This depends on the shelf you have. If your shelves are deep, then go for rectangular folding. If not, square folding will help you save more space. However you may mix it up sometimes so that creases or fold lines won't set in permanently. If possible, refrain from piling too many clothes because excess weight may cause the creases to permanently set in to those clothes at the bottom.

Ensure that shelves are at least 12 inches deep when stacking folded clothes. This is to minimize unused space. Shelves must be well ventilated to prevent growth of molds and presence of pests.

Here's a video showing the simple process of folding shirts....http://bit.ly/17SNgRO

Here's a video showing how to fold a T-shirt in 5 seconds....http://bit.ly/19mD7Kr

Here's a video showing how to save space by Army rolling your T-shirts....http://bit.ly/14nGjaB

Organizing Shoes In Your Closet

Organizing shoes is not as easy as it seems, especially because they can take up a relatively huge space in your closet. Learning how to store them in the most organized and efficient way will help you get over the dilemma whether to put them in the closet or somewhere else in your home.

Shoes may be organized according to their type (E.g. formal shoes, sandals, rubber shoes, and boots). Doing so will save you from the headache of being able to find your shoes in a hurry. It is also practical to place the shoes you frequently use at the most accessible part of the closet. Shoe racks offer great help for you to access your shoes much easier. This can also maximize the space at the bottom part of your closet when nothing is stored in there. Another way of saving closet space is by arranging shoes in the overhead of your closet. You might want to make use of it instead of leaving that space empty.

The physical structure of your closet also plays an important role in determining the type of storing you need to use for your shoes. If your closet has opening doors, you may consider using a hanging shoe rack to maximize space.

Storing shoes in the closet is a convenient way for you to easily access all your clothing needs at once. However, not all conform to this idea because of the chances of spreading dirt into your closet. Smelly shoes, most particularly, are discouraged to be stored inside the closet as it tends to leave the stench in there. After all, who would want a stinky closet?

When storing shoes in the closet, it is advised to put them inside a container in order to keep it dust free and to contain the dirt. Transparent plastic containers are recommended so that you can easily spot the pair of shoes that will best suit your get up. They are also ideal when saving closet space.

For practicality sake, you may use cardboard boxes that come along with your shoes. You do not only save effort but also money. When doing this, pay particular attention to how you stack the boxes. Preferably, you must not go beyond 3 stacks high. If there is really a need to go higher, then you should have an improvised structure that will hold the pile of shoes in place so that the stack won't collapse and the arrangement won't be disturbed whenever you get your shoes from and put them back into the closet.

If you have limited floor space in your closet, going vertical is the best solution. Book casing can be a valuable partner for this. Metro racks can also be used. You may also want to use shoe racks that can be hang on the closet door, the rear wall or on the side walls of your closet.

Remember not to congest your closet with too many shoes. Leave some space for your new acquisitions. Just like clothes, learn to control yourself from hoarding shoes. Those that do not fit you well or those you have not used for a relatively long time must find its new home. You can either donate them to the needy or place them in a box that you can store somewhere else at home.

Never store wet shoes in the closet. Make sure that they are properly dried prior to storage to prevent damage and to keep your closet odor free.

Here's a video showing how to organize your shoes in your closet...http://bit.ly/1aamL8P

Organizing Other Accessories In The Closet

Accessories usually do not consume a lot of space in your closet. However, since they are relatively smaller compared to other items in the closet, they have the tendency to make your closet look like a jungle when not stored properly. More so, due to their small size, accessories can make you go crazy looking for them if they are not properly organized. Like clothes and shoes, accessories are commonly organized according to their type. For women, the usual categories include: bags, jewellery, and belts. For men: ties, belts, and caps. You can further divide them into a more specific category. For example, ties can be organized according to color and style. Jewellery can be organized based on type: earring, necklace, ring, bracelet, and anklet.

Our main goal when organizing the closet is to maximize the use of space. If your closet has shelves, we can maximize the space by putting in dividers. Doing so will allow you to store more items without making any major change in the closet structure. You can also do the same with drawers. When using drawers, you have to make sure that they are placed below eye level so that you can conveniently peep into the items inside. They are more comfortably placed at the waist level so that you do not need to step on a foot stool or stoop down so low.

Hooks are also trusted allies when it comes to storing your accessories such as belts, bags, scarves, and ties. If the side walls, back wall, or the inside part of the opening doors of your closet are left unused, then you can fully utilize those spaces by hanging your accessories using hooks. This is a very cheap and easy way of organizing. However, you have to consider hanging only a single item on each hook to allow more efficient usage. If you hang more than one item on a single hook, the consequence is that you have to take all items from the hook before you can get the one you're looking for. Then you have to put the rest back onto the hook again. But if you really lack space and decide to place more than one item on a single hook, then you have to learn to be patient when taking and putting back the items. Besides what's important is that you have maximized the space in your closet.

When storing your precious jewellery, use small containers. Avoid mixing your jewellery with other items especially sharp objects because this may cause scratches and dents. Transparent plastic containers are recommended in order to allow easy visualization of your jewellery in order to save time and effort when looking for them.

PVC pipes that have at least 6-inch diameter can be used as well in organizing your accessories. This is a very practical and clever way in saving space. You may store your rolled socks, face towels, and the like in the pipe.

Here's a guide on how to fold your socks.

Lay down your socks on a clean surface (e.g. the bed) and place one sock over the other.

Fold 2 socks into half.

Hold one end in pace then pull the other end gently.

Roll the socks going to the open end. Gently pull while rolling the socks.

Using your dominant hand, hold the rolled socks as if you are holding a soda in can.

Insert the thumb of your dominant hand into the opening of the sock.

Pull the garter backwards, thus, covering the roll of sock. Do necessary adjustments.

There may be other items left unmentioned in this article but the same principle applies when storing them. You may simply put a plastic box in your closet where you can place items left in your pocket. Taking out these small stuff is important because when they are left in the pocket and accidentally included in the laundry, it might cause damage in your pants. It can either stain or tear your pants. The worse is, they can even ruin your washing machine. Save yourself from all these troubles by taking this simple step.

Here's a video showing how to organize your accessories in your closet...http://bit.ly/15CpMjZ

Here's a video showing how to organize your bags and purses in your closet...http://bit.ly/13kruTt

Here's a video showing how to organize your jewellery...http://bit.ly/152CbLR

How to Keep An Organized Closet Organized

Organizing closet is undeniably a challenging task. It's terribly difficult at the beginning but it is equally and sometimes even more difficult when it comes to maintaining your closet in proper order. This is true especially at times when you are in a hurry. Your adrenaline rush tends to blind you from keeping your closet neat and tidy.

The main key to keep your closet organized is to establish self-discipline. Make it a habit to never leave your closet in chaos. When taking out folded clothes, do not abruptly pull the item out. Insert your non-dominant hand (with palm facing upward) above the clothing to be taken, slightly lift the stack of clothes while your dominant hand gently pulls the chosen item. Do the same with any of your folded stuff.

Leaving the closet disorganized in order not to be late is never an acceptable reason. Allot ample time for preparation. If there are inevitable circumstances, make sure to reorganize your closet right away upon arriving at home. Closets that are left disorganized in a couple of days make you vulnerable to become complacent. You'll be exhausted having the mere thought of doing the same "closet organizing" thing again. Prevent this from happening by developing a 5-minute closet aftercare before leaving your room. Try practicing this for 14 consecutive days and unknowingly, it becomes a part of your routine. The next time you do it, it's already effortless.

Another major root cause of a chaotic closet is the continuously increasing number of items inside of it that can no longer be contained. The rule for this problem is simple: stop hoarding!

It may sound easy but the fact is it's not, especially when you get so attached with your stuff. However, put in mind that there's always an end in every journey. Start tossing your other stuff by following simple rules.

First step: ASSESSMENT. Ask yourself these basic questions:

What types of clothing do I need or use the most?

What clothes make me feel and look good?

What clothes represent the real me?

All those clothes answering these three basic questions are the ones that must stay in your closet. The rest that do not answer the questions must be subject for re-assessment. Make a little exemption for the clothes which hold sentimental value to you but do not hoard them all. Keep an item or two that hold significant relevance to you.

Second step: DIAGNOSE. Identify the main reason why you came up with too many items in your closet. Basically, these are the two main culprits of a clutter-filled closet.

Hoarding too much

Buying too much

Third step: PLANNING. Plan how to address the identified problem above. Be SMART when formulating your plan. SMART stands for:

(S) Specific. Be very particular in setting your goal. Example: "I will only keep those clothes I have been frequently using for the past 6 months."

(M) Measurable. Set a quantifiable measure for the number of clothes that can be ideally stored in your closet. You have to take into consideration the dimensions of your closet, the shelves, drawers, tracks, and others. If your closet space can only accommodate 20 hanging clothes and 50 folded clothes, then keep that as a standard. Do not go beyond that number.

(AR) Attainable and Realistic. Commit to the fulfilment of your plan. If 50 clothes must only stay in the shelves, then do it. Do not bend your rules so easily.

(T) Time-bounded. Do it at the soonest possible time. The longer time you waste, the less enthusiastic you will become.

Fourth step: IMPLEMENTATION. Whatever is the result of your planning phase, it must be executed. Do not end in planning or else everything will be put to waste. Here are some suggested actions.

If you hoard too much, then this is the perfect time to learn to donate some of your stuff. If you're not so sure about giving them away, you can perhaps store them in a box somewhere else in your home.

Another very interesting way of letting go of your stuff is by earning an income from them. This is a very nice way of disposing your unused stuff. It's like hitting two birds with one stone. You declutter your closet and at the same time, make a little bit of money at the same time.

If you buy too much, then perhaps next time you have to learn to contemplate before buying clothes. Ask yourself if you really need it. Do not just buy items because they look stunning. Not everything that looks stunning would make you look stunning.

Fifth step: Evaluation. After doing all the suggested actions above, ask yourself these questions:

Are all my objectives met?

If yes, what should I do to maintain my closet organized?

If no, what could have been the reason? What should have I done?

For an unsuccessful attempt, try to reformulate your plan. There could be something more to include. Decluttering your closet can be done monthly or even weekly. The more often you do it, the less effort you need to exert. You must also bear in mind not to commit the common mistakes when organizing your closet in order to prevent clutter.

The very basic reason of a messy ending is a not well-planned beginning. Before attempting to organize the closet, you must have a SMART plan. You must have a clear picture of what you want to achieve in the end, of what you want your closet to look like. Another culprit is "doing before thinking". Purchasing organizing products without the definite plan on how to use them leads you to a "come what may" style of organizing. In the end, your closet becomes a disaster. If not, you just wasted your money to something you do not need.

Avoid placing your items somewhere else. Put back the ties where they are supposed to be stored. Even if you have the most grandiose shoe rack in the whole world, if you do not put your shoes back in it, its purpose is defeated and your closet becomes a tragedy.

A lot of people tend to develop a syndrome manifested by the statement: "I might use it in time." Who knows when will that be? Or will you ever reach that time? Hoarding stuff because of the hope of using them in the future is not a wise idea. Give or sell it to someone who needs it more.

One of the most efficient ways to keep your closet organized is by letting other family members know how your system works. This is true especially among couples sharing the same closet. You will grow tired of reorganizing your closet over and over again while your partner does exactly the opposite. In the end, you'll find yourself doing what he/she is doing. Orient others about your system and influence them to do the same in their own closet.
A lot of efforts have been exerted just for you to come up with an organized closet. Do not let your efforts go to waste!

Organizing your closet tips videos
http://bit.ly/1aanhDZ
http://bit.ly/19mE8lO
http://bit.ly/14nHxTc

Additional Tips In Organizing Your Closet

Apart from clothing, some people have other stuff in their closets especially if they own a large closet. Commonly included items are old photo albums, CDs, and even school or office files. Just like your clothes, you have to learn to throw out these items that are no longer needed.

Some of us are fond of keeping our school files thinking that someday we can show our kids how well we performed in school. I used to hoard all my quizzes and examination booklets in college until such time I noticed that they are consuming much space in my closet plus the dust that accumulates in the file case makes the rest of my closet dusty. That's when I realized that the more stuff you keep, the more dust you also keep. So I simply took out all my college files and started sorting important from unimportant papers. Since those quiz papers and examination booklets hold sentimental value to me, I decided to take a picture of them before finally disposing them. That's the end of it. With the kind of technology we have today, keeping the actual item for sentimental reasons is not anymore practical. Try saving a few then take a photo of the rest.

If your closet is too congested, you may consider placing other stuff in a plastic storage box. Plastic boxes are recommended over cardboard boxes because the former usually last longer and they are more pleasing to the eye than the latter. Don't forget to properly label the boxes so you do not need to open them just to check what's inside.

Oftentimes, we mistakenly see our closets as a storage place. It's definitely not! So if you happen to see empty boxes of perfume, shoes, etc. in your closet, take them out and stack them somewhere else. Your closet is not the proper place for them. There are some who develop the habit of keeping empty containers in the closet hoping that they could use those stuff in the future. Store them somewhere else because what must be stored in the closet are items you need today and not in the future. This must be given emphasis to all hoarders out there.

Since we have established the fact that closets are not storage places, it's time to prove it by making your closet look different from your storage room. Aside from organizing things properly, add some spice to the look of your closet by decorating it according to your preference. The closet is your personal space that should make you feel good and comfortable. You can paint it with your favorite color. You can add mirrors, pegboards, or even corkboards where you can pin your own images, photos of your favorite celebrity, reminders, etc. Decorate your closet as if you are in a salon, a boutique shop, or elsewhere. Excite yourself with the idea of changing your closet mood at least every year.

Furthermore, you also need to identify any additional needs for your closet. If you have a relatively huge space in your closet that can still accommodate your used clothes, then you might want to consider putting your hampers in there. This will save your time and effort from going to the laundry area whenever you get undressed. If possible, provide two hampers; one for your white clothes and the other for your colored clothes.

It is quite uncomfortable to pull a chair from your room every time you wear your shoes. If there is still space in the closet, you might want to consider putting a small chair in it. Another thing you should include in your closet is a plastic bin that will contain your small stuff like keys, coins, or candies that usually get left inside your pocket. Take them out of the pocket before they end up in the washing machine.

Another issue we face when talking about closets is mutual sharing. It's quite difficult to maintain an organized closet when more than one person uses it. The prime rule for this one is that both must commit to keep their closet organized at all times. If one practices the 5-minute after care policy, then the other one must also do the same. Harmony and cooperation is an essential component when sharing a closet.

Equally divide the space in your closet. Allot specific areas and identify who consumes this and that space. Make your closet organizing time a bonding moment. This will help strengthen your relationship as a couple.

Closet sharing is not only applicable to couples. If you have brothers and/or sisters, you can also share closet with them. Parents must train their children how to organize their closets. This will enable their children to develop a sense of responsibility and accountability.

The benefits of having an organized closet are way immeasurable. A disorganized closet is an eyesore that can ruin your entire day. When you see something chaotic, you get upset. Your mood changes when you get upset. Instead of waking up to a beautiful day, you end up having a bad day the moment you open your closet doors because your chaotic closet has consumed your positive vibes. That's the psychological impact of a disorganized closet.

Having a well-organized closet enables you to dress up and groom more efficiently. It will save you from the hassle of looking for your stuff. You can readily access your clothes and accessories because you know exactly where you store them. There's no reason to get late to work because you can quickly access your needed items.

Everything really seems difficult at the beginning but when you get used to it then it becomes effortless the next time you do it. Start organizing your closet today while the enthusiasm and the spirit are still up. But don't get too excited to the extent that you forgot to plan and directly started taking everything out of the closet.

Good luck on your closet endeavors!

Tips on how to organize a family closet
http://bit.ly/152CHJw

How to fold clothes and organize drawers in your closet…http://bit.ly/14uT7qv

Do it yourself closet organization
http://bit.ly/15H64Nb

24164867R00026

Made in the USA
Lexington, KY
19 December 2018